WHO COMES FIRST?

Elizabeth Burra

Illustrated by
Pamela Dormer

D1739826

Scripture Union,
47 Marylebone Lane, London W1M 6AX

Photoset in Malta,
by St Paul's Press Ltd

Printed in Great Britain by
A. McLay & Co. Ltd. Cardiff and London

Contents

The Prince Who Ran Away

Pharaoh, the King of Egypt, was worried. For weeks he had lain awake in bed at night turning the problem over in his mind. And what was the problem? It was those Hebrew people. They had been living in Egypt for many years. Generations of them had worked hard in the land and gradually their little colony had grown and grown. It wasn't that they were doing Pharaoh any harm or causing him any trouble. They worked hard, paid their taxes and really kept themselves to themselves.

All the same, Pharaoh was worried. What if there should be a war? It was just possible that the Hebrews might take sides with Egypt's enemies, then the Egyptians would really be in trouble. Pharaoh had even made the Hebrews into slaves. They were not allowed to work and live as they wanted to, but had to work for the Egyptians.

Men called taskmasters were appointed to make sure that the Hebrews always worked hard. They had to carry heavy loads of bricks and mortar which were used for building. As the hot sun beat down on them they grew very tired and unhappy, but still the task masters were there to make sure they worked as hard as ever and to whip them if they did not.

You might think that the Hebrew people would be worn down by this treatment. But not a bit of it. The women seemed to have even more babies and the colony continued to grow. When Pharaoh saw that more and more Hebrew babies were being born he decided to issue a terrible command. He ordered the midwives to kill all the boy babies born to the Hebrew women and to allow only the girls to live. Of course, the midwives did not want to do this so they let the boy babies live and then made excuses to Pharaoh.

What *could* Pharaoh do? He talked over the problem with his advisers and then made his decision. He gave an order that the Egyptian people had to throw all the Hebrew baby boys into the river.

The Hebrews were dismayed. Mothers cuddled their babies to them and trembled at the thought of having them snatched away and thrown into the river. There was one mother who looked at the beautiful baby boy in her arms and knew that, whatever happened, she could not let him be drowned.

This mother, her husband and the baby's older sister, Miriam, whispered together as they planned how they could save the baby. Then they thought of a wonderful idea. The mother made a little boat of papyrus reeds and daubed it with tar to make it waterproof. Gently she put the baby in the little boat, placed a cover over him so that he was completely hidden, and laid the boat among the reeds that grew by the edge of the river.

Miriam stayed on the bank of the river and kept

watch over the little boat so that she could see what happened to her baby brother. Then she noticed a group of women walking along the river bank. One of them was beautifully dressed in a long silk dress and golden jewelry. The others, who were not so well dressed, seemed to be her maids as they were carrying her belongings.

As they came nearer, Miriam recognised her as one of Pharaoh's daughters, an Egyptian princess. Miriam stood very still so that they shouldn't see her. Then she held her breath and just stopped herself from crying out as she saw the princess pointing to the little boat where the baby was lying.

Miriam's heart sank as she saw one of the maids go towards the floating cradle. Surely her brother would now be discovered and thrown into the river. The maid took the cradle over to the princess who lifted off the top. There was the baby, crying for food and warmth and someone to love him.

'He must be one of the Hebrew children,' said the princess. She knew what her father had commanded, she knew that she should throw the baby into the river but, when she looked at him crying in his little cradle, she knew that she could not drown him.

Miriam looked on from her hiding place. When she saw the concern on the princess's face a tiny flicker of hope came to her. It seemed a crazy suggestion, but it was worth trying. Stepping out into the open, she went up to the group of women and spoke to the princess.

'Shall I find one of the Hebrew women to nurse him for you?' she asked.

The princess thought for a moment, then said, 'Yes, do.'

Miriam ran all the way back home to bring her mother and, when the two returned, the princess made arrangements to pay the woman to look after the baby, her own baby!

Perhaps you already know the name of the baby. He was called Moses. After such an exciting beginning to his life, many more exciting things were to happen to him.

Back in his own simple home, Moses was looked after by his mother and father and sister. He learnt that life wasn't easy when your people were slaves. Often his father would come in exhausted after a day's work, far too tired to play with his son.

There were very few other boys for him to play with either. Moses wondered why, but it seemed that something awful had happened to them, something that grown ups whispered about when he was there, something that he might learn about when he was older.

Although they were poor and life was hard, Moses was very happy. He loved to sit and listen to his mother telling stories about great leaders of the Hebrews, men like Joseph, who had first come to Egypt as a slave many years ago and then had become a powerful government official. Moses also learnt about God, who had promised to help the Hebrew people. He learnt to know God for himself and he began to learn a bit about how God wanted his people to live.

The years passed quickly and soon the day came

when Moses' mother had to take him to the palace to give him back to the princess who had spared his life. Now there was a dramatic change in Moses' life. At first he was upset at having to leave the home where he had lived so happily. He was bewildered by his strange, new surroundings. He had to dress in fine, rich clothes and eat expensive food. The palace was so big that it was easy to get lost. The people even spoke a different language!

The princess was kind to him, though, and treated him just as if he were her own son. Gradually, as he became more used to his new way of life, Moses began to find it quite exciting. He played with the Egyptian boys of the court and went to school, where he learnt maths and science and many other interesting subjects.

As he grew up, Moses enjoyed his life as an Egyptian prince. He was popular, had all that money could buy, and looked forward to a bright future. But, although it seemed a very long time since he had lived with his own Hebrew parents, Moses could never forget that really he was a Hebrew and not an Egyptian. It was something he often wished he could forget, because he knew that to stand up and be loyal to the Hebrews could mean trouble for him.

It could mean that he would have to give up many things he enjoyed: his wealth, his gay social life and the way people looked up to him as a prince of Egypt. But he knew, too, that God, his God, was with the Hebrew people. He knew that to turn his back on them would be to turn his back on God.

He had to decide what to do. He thought about it for many weeks. Then he made up his mind. His loyalty must lie with his own Hebrew people and with their God.

One day he went to the place where the Hebrews were working. He saw the terrible conditions. He saw how hard they were made to work. Then he saw an Egyptian taskmaster knocking one of the Hebrew men to the ground. This was more than Moses could bear to watch. Quickly he looked round to see that no one was looking then went straight over to the taskmaster and killed him. He hurriedly buried the body in the sand and left, hoping that no one had seen what had happened.

Back at the palace, Moses sat down to think. He was horrified by what he had done. He had been so reckless, so stupid. Killing the taskmaster had not helped his people. When, next day, he learnt that some men had seen what had happened, he panicked. If Pharaoh heard of it, Moses would really be in trouble. Pharaoh did find out. He gave orders for Moses to be arrested and executed but Moses escaped, left Egypt and went to live in the land of Midian.

The decision he had made did not seem to have got Moses very far. Here he was, living in a foreign land, miles away from his own people. He married a Midianite girl and worked for his father-in-law looking after his sheep.

Then, one day, when Moses was out shepherding on some rough scrub land at the foot of a mountain, he saw something that stopped him dead in his

tracks. There was a bush which seemed to be on fire, but which was not being burnt away. God was making this happen and He spoke to Moses very clearly. Moses listened in amazement as God told him that he was going to send him back to Egypt to see Pharaoh, and that Moses was to demand that Pharaoh should let him lead the Hebrew people out of Egypt. It seemed impossible to Moses. Of course he wanted his people to be free, but the thought of standing in front of Pharaoh terrified him. He tried to argue with God and make excuses, but God assured him He would be with Moses and the plan would succeed.

So Moses went back to Egypt, with his brother, Aaron whom God had sent to meet Moses and to go with him. They asked Pharaoh to let the people go, but he refused and so God proved that he was the helper of the Hebrews by sending terrible plagues to the Egyptians.

The rivers were turned to blood so that the water could no longer be used for drinking; there were plagues of frogs and lice and flies all over the land. The cattle belonging to the Egyptians became ill and died, but the cattle owned by the Hebrews remained strong. You might think that Pharoah would have been glad to let the Hebrews go, but somehow, as soon as each plague had gone, he changed his mind. So God had to send even more plagues. There were boils that covered the bodies of the Egyptian people as well as their animals. There was a terrible hailstorm which ruined the crops. There was a storm of locusts, insects which ate all the leaves they came to and left the trees and fields bare. And then there was darkness, not a speck of light for the Egyptians to see to do anything.

Last of all, God sent an angel of death to kill the oldest boy in every Egyptian family. Pharaoh's eldest son died, too. Sadly Pharaoh realised that he could not fight against God. He would have to let the Hebrew people go.

Hurriedly, the Hebrew families gathered together their belongings. Mothers, fathers, grandparents, young children, everyone was going.

What excitement there was as they set off, leaving the land where they had been slaves for so long. And at the head of the procession went Moses, their loyal leader.

Far Away from Home

In a little town called Bethlehem lived a man called Elimelech. He was a farmer. And he was a descendent of those Hebrew slaves who had left Egypt, travelled to Canaan, and after many adventures and difficulties, settled down peacefully to farm the land.

Elimelech was married to Naomi, who had given him two fine sons, and the little family were very happy together. Bethlehem was the sort of little town where everyone seemed to know everyone else and so, even when her husband was away at work, Naomi had plenty of friends and relations nearby, always ready to chat and so she never felt lonely.

One year, however, Elimelech began to look worried. He knew that the crops of corn were likely to fail, and the thought of what that meant made him shudder. As the year went by there was scarcely any golden corn to be cut down with long scythes and then threshed to separate the grain from the outer husks. Naomi's store of grain grew smaller and smaller and each week she could bake less bread than the week before.

Elimelech grew desperate as he looked at his family growing thinner and thinner and he knew about the pangs of hunger that his wife and two boys were suffering. They must do *something*. They could not stay and starve to death. Then some news began to spread around the town. Far away to the South, in the land of Moab, there had been good crops. If Elimelech and his family could reach that land they would be able to eat well again.

It was with mixed feelings that Naomi helped her husband to pack up ready for the journey. Of course there was the hope of food once they reached the land of Moab, but leaving their home meant leaving many of their friends and relatives. It also meant taking with them as many of their possessions as possible for they did not know if they would ever be coming back to the land of Israel.

They travelled for several weeks, not by themselves but with other families who had also decided to leave behind their empty fields and to start a new life in another land. The roads were rough and the travellers grew very tired as they walked day after day with only a few pack mules to help to carry all their belongings. One day though, their journey did come to an end and they were able to put down their packs and begin to settle down to their new life in Moab.

Several years passed and Elimelech and Naomi grew used to their new home. It had been a relief to come to a land where they could once again have all the corn they needed to eat well every day, but there had been many things to learn. The people in Moab spoke a different language to them, they dressed and worked and lived in a different way and, most important of all, they did not worship the one true living God of Israel, but instead worshipped lots of gods whom they imagined to be real but who did not really exist at all.

The family had not long settled down in their new land when something very sad happened to them. Elimelech died, leaving Naomi a widow to bring up her two sons. It was a struggle but Naomi worked hard and was a good mother. The years passed quickly until the two boys grew up and married. Naomi was pleased to see them settled down with good wives, and grew fond of her daughters-in-law, Ruth and Orpah, even though they were Moabite girls and not from her own land of Israel.

Naomi's happiness did not last long though, for, not long after they married, both sons died and Naomi, Ruth and Orpah were now all widows. With the death of her sons as well as her husband Naomi began to feel a lonely ache inside her. She felt more and more lost in the land of Moab and started to think of her home in Bethlehem which she had left so long ago. When she heard that once again there had been good crops in Bethlehem she made up her mind that she would make the long journey back, and take Orpah and Ruth with her.

The sad little party set off on the journey back to Bethlehem but, after they had gone a little way, Naomi began to think. Was it really fair to take her daughters-in-law with her to the land of Israel? They would be just as much strangers there as she had been in Moab. Perhaps it would be better for them to go back to their own country where they might find second husbands amongst their own people.

Finally she said to them, 'Why don't you return to your parents' homes instead of coming with me? And may the Lord reward you for your faithfulness to your husbands and to me. And may he bless you with another happy marriage.' Then she kissed them goodbye.

All three of the women began to cry. They did not want to leave each other and Orpah and Ruth said that they still wanted to go on with Naomi. But Naomi was insistent. She had no younger sons whom they could marry and it would be much better for them to go back and find happiness in their own land than to carry on for the sake of being with her. Finally Orpah agreed to go back. She kissed Naomi goodbye and went to live with her own parents in Moab.

But Ruth had come to love Naomi and wanted to stay with her, whatever happened. She wanted to belong to Naomi's people, the people of Israel, and she knew about the God of Israel whom Naomi worshipped and she wanted to worship Him too. When Naomi saw that Ruth had really made up her mind to stay with her, the two women carried on together back to Bethlehem.

You can imagine the stir their arrival caused in the little town of Bethlehem. Although Naomi had been away so long some people still recognised her and, as the news spread around the town that she was back, people came to say 'Hello' and to catch up on all the news of what had happened since she had left so long ago. It must have been good for Naomi to be back among so many friends and relations, even though she was still feeling sad.

Without husbands to work for them in the fields, Naomi and Ruth had a hard struggle to find food to eat. Poor people who did not have fields of their own were sometimes able to get corn by walking behind the reapers who were gathering in the corn, and picking up any ears of corn that were dropped or left behind. This was called gleaning.

One day Ruth was gleaning in a field when the owner of the field arrived to see how his workers were getting on. When he saw Ruth he asked his foreman who she was and the foreman explained that Ruth was the girl who had come back from the land of Moab with Naomi. The foreman told the owner, whose name was Boaz, how Ruth had asked him if she could glean in the field and how she had been working there nearly all day.

Boaz was touched by the sight of this young woman working so hard in the blazing sun. He knew how loyal she had been to Naomi in staying with her even though it meant leaving her own country, and he knew too what kindness she had shown. He called her over and told her that she could stay in his fields to glean and that she need not bother to go anywhere else. She could help herself to the water there too whenever she was thirsty. At lunch-time, Ruth was invited to eat with the men and Boaz gave her so much food that she could not eat it all, so she took

what was left home with her that night and gave it to Naomi.

It was not only the remains of her lunch that she was able to take to Naomi that night. Boaz had told his men that, when they were reaping, they should break off some ears of corn on purpose and let them fall to the ground so that Ruth could glean them. When she came to thresh the corn she found that she had such a big pile of grain that she could hardly carry it home.

Naomi was delighted when she saw how much grain Ruth had and Ruth was eager to tell her about everything that had happened that day. When she mentioned that the owner of the field was called Boaz, Naomi could hardly believe it. Boaz was one of her closest relatives! She was so thankful to God for Boaz' kindness.

Ruth went back to Boaz' fields until all the harvest was finished and so she and Naomi had plenty of grain to make into bread. But that was not all, for before very long Boaz and Ruth married and had a baby son. Naomi was thrilled to have a grandson of her own and, as she looked at her daughter-in-law holding her baby son, she was very pleased that Ruth, who had been so loyal to her, should now be so happy herself.

Two Good Friends

When Jonathan was still a teenager, something happened that could only happen in *your* wildest dreams. His father became King, the King of Israel. Even though he was now a prince, Jonathan's life was hard and dangerous. There were many enemies of the Israelites living around them and often there were battles to fight.

Jonathan was young when he learnt how to fight. Soon he was leading attacks against Israel's enemies, the Philistines. He was a good soldier but he knew that by itself that was not enough. As he grew up he came to know God and to trust him for help.

Jonathan's father, King Saul, had also trusted God when he was first made King. But he did not always do what God wanted him to do. One day an old man called Samuel came to see Saul. He had some bad news for him.

'Because you have not done what God told you to do,' he said, 'God does not want you to be King any more.'

What a blow for Saul! He could hardly believe his ears. Although he would be able to carry on acting as King until he died, Saul would not have the joy of knowing that the kingship would then pass to his son, Jonathan.

After that Saul became very depressed and frightened. His helpers were worried about him. What could they do to make him feel cheerful again? Then someone had an idea. Why not have some soothing music? That was just what would help Saul. Another helper said he knew just the person who could play for Saul. There was a young man called David who was a very talented musician. 'What is more,' the servant added, 'he's a sensible chap, a brave fighter and God is with him.'

And so David started to play for Saul from time to time and the lovely, lilting music would help to make Saul feel happier. Jonathan heard about this young musician who was playing for his father. 'It would be good to meet him,' he thought. But in fact they did not meet until after David had had a wonderful adventure.

The Philistine army had a huge giant of a man on their side. He was called Goliath. The Philistine and Israelite armies were camping on opposite sides of a valley and, each morning, Goliath would come out and challenge one person from the Israelites to fight him. If Goliath won the fight then the Philistine army would have the victory. As the Israelites looked mournfully across at this huge man their fate seemed certain. Surely they would never be able to find anyone big and strong enough to face Goliath.

David's three oldest brothers were in the Israelite army. One day David's father sent him to take food to them and to see how they were getting on. They told him about Goliath and how the whole army was afraid of him. And, went on one brother, 'Saul has offered a reward to any man who will kill the giant. He will be able to marry one of Saul's daughters, and his family won't have to pay taxes for a whole year!'

That sounded good. But there was something more important than reward. God had promised to be with the Israelite army. How dare this Philistine set himself up against God's army?

David made up his mind that he would kill Goliath. Armed only with a bag of stones and a sling, he walked out on to the field. Goliath was scornful. Who did this boy think he was? But his scorn didn't last long for *God* was helping David. Carefully David put a stone into his sling then, taking aim, he flung it at Goliath. With a thud the huge man fell to the ground, dead. The stone had sunk right into his forehead.

All the Israelite soldiers were overjoyed. Now their enemy was defeated. David was a real hero and Saul sent for him to have a talk. After that he introduced him to Jonathan. As soon as he met David, Jonathan knew that they were going to be friends. He was thrilled when his father said that David could stay with them. Everyone was delighted, too, when Saul made David commander of the troops.

The friendship between David and Jonathan grew stronger every day. But Saul began to grow uneasy. The people seemed to love David more than they loved him. And God was always with David, helping him in everything he did. But God had abandoned Saul altogether since he had been disobedient. Saul became very jealous of David. He began to hate him so much that he wanted to kill him. One day, as

David was playing the harp, Saul threw his spear at him. David just managed to leap out of the way in time.

Saul didn't give up. When he heard that Michal, his daughter, had fallen in love with David, he made another plan to kill him. He sent for David.

'You can marry Michal,' he said, 'if you go out and kill two hundred Philistines.'

'Now,' Saul thought, 'David is bound to be killed in the fighting.' But David wasn't killed and, instead, he was happily married.

With every unsuccessful effort to kill David, Saul grew more and more jealous. He tried to murder him on several occasions but Jonathan and Michal helped David to escape death. Eventually David could stand Saul's hatred no longer. He found Jonathan by himself.

'Why is your father trying to kill me?', David blurted out.

But Jonathan had not yet heard of Saul's latest attempt on David's life. He looked puzzled. 'I'm sure he would have told me what he was planning,' he said.

'Of course he wouldn't!' exclaimed David. 'He knows what good friends we are. He wouldn't want to hurt you by telling you he was planning to kill me.'

Jonathan grew worried. He must find out definitely what Saul was planning. David and he needed to make their plan too. He wanted to be loyal to his friend, whatever happened.

'You know I will do anything to help you,' he said.

David thought for a moment, then he had an idea. 'Tomorrow is the beginning of the Feast of the New Moon,' he said. 'I usually spend that feast with your father but, this time, I'll hide in the field outside instead. He's bound to miss me if I am not at the feast. Will you tell him that I've gone to see my own relations? Then, if he seems pleased, we'll know that all is well, but, if he's angry about me not being there, then we'll know he is planning to kill me.'

That sounded a good idea. Jonathan readily agreed to the plan. Then David thought of another problem.

'How will I know if your father is angry or not?', he wondered.

This time Jonathan had the answer. 'If you hide over there, by that pile of stones, I'll come out into the field on the third day of the feast and shoot three arrows just in front of the pile as if I was using it for a target. I'll bring a boy out with me and, when I've shot the arrows, I'll send him to fetch them. If you hear me shout to him that the arrows are on this side, then you'll know that everything is all right. But, if I say to him, "Go farther – the arrows are still ahead of you," then that will mean that Saul is angry and you will have to leave as quickly as possible.'

So, the next day, David took up his hiding position. Jonathan went in to the celebration feast. David's empty place looked so obvious. Why didn't his father comment on it? But Saul thought there must be a good reason for David not being there. He was sure he would turn up for the second day of the feast. The second day came and still David's place was empty.

'Why hasn't David been here yesterday or today?' Saul asked.

Jonathan took a deep breath. 'He asked if he could go to his family re-union,' he replied.

Saul was furious. He told Jonathan to bring David so that he could kill him. But Jonathan defended his friend.

'He hasn't done any wrong. Why should he be killed?' he exclaimed.

Now Saul was so angry that, hardly knowing what he was doing, he picked up his spear and hurled it at his son. Jonathan jumped out of the way and ran from the room. When he got his breath back he thought things over. 'It really looks as though my father is going out of his mind with worry and jealousy,' he thought. 'I'd better keep out of his way until he calms down.'

Jonathan knew now that it would not be safe for David to stay in the Palace. He must carry out the plan they had devised. It might mean angering his father even more, but Jonathan wanted his friend's safety to come first.

So, on the third morning of the feast, Jonathan went into the field with his bow and arrows just as he and David had arranged. David watched from his hiding place as Jonathan shot three arrows. Then he held his breath. What would the message be? With a thumping heart he heard his friend shout, 'The arrows are still ahead of you.' Now he knew the worst. Saul still wanted to kill him. He would have to flee. Jonathan sent the boy away, then he rushed over to his friend.

Tears streamed down their faces as the two friends said goodbye. They did not know when they might see each other again. David would miss his loyal friend very much in the dangerous months that lay ahead. But they gave each other into God's care, and that was the best thing they could have done.

One Man – and God

Ahab, the king of Israel, had married the most dreadful wife you can imagine. His kingdom was smaller than King David's, because there had been quarrels and wars and the country that David had ruled was now divided into two kingdoms, Israel in the north and Judah in the south.

When King Ahab had married Jezebel, things had started to go seriously wrong again. Jezebel was one of those people who always want their own way. She was very cruel and mean and, to make matters worse, she knew just how to wrap her husband round her little finger. She could make him do just what she wanted.

Jezebel worshipped Baal, who some people thought was the god of the sun. These people thought that if you wanted good crops of corn, plenty of ripe fruit and strong cattle then you had to give presents to Baal. They gave these presents, or sacrifices as they were called, at special ceremonies. At these ceremonies everyone often ended up getting very drunk.

Sometimes they burnt sweet-smelling incense as a present to Baal. Sometimes they killed an animal and burnt it. Sometimes mothers and fathers would even kill one of their children and burn him. All this to worship a god who was not even really there! It was all very sad. Now you can see why God was so angry when the King had been persuaded by his wife to worship Baal and, what was more, many of the people of Israel had followed the example of their king.

But there was one man who had not started to worship Baal. He was one of the men who had remained loyal to God. This man was called Elijah. Elijah had grown up in the country, far from the nearest town. He had spent most of his time out of doors and this had made him strong and fit with skin as brown as a berry. During the long days that Elijah had spent alone in the hills he had been able to get to know God as his friend and he had come to know when God was talking to him.

Now the time came when God decided that the people of Israel should be punished because they had started to worship Baal. Something very dreadful happened. Elijah announced that there would be no rain for several years. Can you imagine what that meant? There was not enough water to drink and both the people and the animals grew thirsty. The crops could not grow without rain and so there was not enough food to eat. The people were so hungry and thirsty that many of them became ill or died.

One day King Ahab and one of his chief men, called Obadiah, set off to try to find water for the King's horses. They decided they would split up and the King would go one way and Obadiah would go another, so that they would have a better chance of finding water. As Obadiah was going along the road he saw a man walking towards him. Who could this be? It was Elijah. God had sent him on a very special errand.

Elijah sent Obadiah to tell the King that he had come, and so King Ahab came out to meet Elijah. The wicked King was very angry when he saw Elijah and he blamed *him* for the fact that there had been no rain. But Elijah knew the real reason for the drought. He told the King that the reason there had been no rain was because he and his family had refused to obey God and had worshipped Baal instead.

Then he gave the King some instructions. All the people of Israel, many thousands of them, had to go to Mount Carmel. Four hundred and fifty of the prophets of Baal and another four hundred prophets who supported Queen Jezebel had to go too. King Ahab sent messages to all the people telling them to go to Mount Carmel. They had no idea what was going to happen when they arrived, but they felt sure that it must be something very important.

As they set off early in the morning everyone must have been very excited. As they met other groups of people all heading for Mount Carmel they talked excitedly. Would some miracle happen? They hardly dared hope that the rain which was needed so badly would fall once again. Then through the crowd that had now gathered on the mountain came the King. Everyone moved to one side to make a gap for him to pass through. He didn't walk like everyone else but was carried by four strong men on a sort of wooden bed called a litter. Now the wicked

31

King Ahab had arrived. The prophets of Baal were there and the people of Israel were all waiting to see what would happen.

Suddenly everyone grew quiet and all eyes turned in one direction as up the hill walked a tall, bronzed man. Here was Elijah, a man who had stayed loyal to God when so many others had worshipped Baal. The prophets of Baal looked at him with hatred. What could one man do against so many? Having got everyone up on the mountain, what was he going to do next?

Elijah then spoke to all the people. He told them that they had to make up their minds. If the Lord God of Israel was really God then they must follow him, but if Baal was God, then they should follow him. Then he told them to bring two young bulls. The four hundred and fifty prophets of Baal could choose which one they wanted, kill it and place it on an altar. The Elijah would take the other young bull and place it on another altar. Each altar would have plenty of wood on it but no fire underneath.

'Then,' said Elijah, 'you prophets of Baal can pray to your god, and I will pray to the Lord God of Israel and whichever god answers by sending fire to burn the wood on the altar, then he must be the True God.'

The people all thought that this was a fair test and agreed to the plan. Elijah told the prophets of Baal that they could go first. After all, there were many more of them. So they prepared the bull and put it on their altar, after which they began to pray to Baal. The people watched, holding their breath to

see what would happen. Nothing did. The prophets began to dance round the altar, they shouted to Baal now, they cut themselves with knives and swords to show just how much they wanted Baal to answer, but still nothing happened.

At last Elijah called the people over to where there had once been an altar to the Lord. It had been broken down, but now he began to repair it. Then he placed the wood on it and finally placed the young bull on top. Elijah was so sure that God would answer his prayer and send the fire even if the wood was wet that he told some men to pour big barrels of water over the wood. Now no one could say that he had cheated.

Elijah then prayed to God, 'Prove today that you are the God of Israel.' When he had finished praying a tremendous flash of fire came down from heaven. The flames burnt the wood, the young bull and the whole of the altar.

All the people were amazed when they saw what had happened. They knew now who was the true God; they fell to the ground and bowed their faces into the dust because they wanted to worship the living God who had answered Elijah's prayer in such a wonderful way. How sorry they must have felt that they had ever been persuaded to worship Baal and to disobey the true God.

The prophets of Baal were all killed so that they could never again stop people worshipping God. Elijah knew now that God would once again send rain and he told King Ahab that there would soon be a huge rainstorm. The King drove quickly to the nearest town. He felt ashamed of the way he had treated God and his prophet, Elijah. He knew now which God he should worship. But what about Jezebel? He hated to think how she would react when he told her what had happened. Sure enough, Jezebel was furious and, far from asking God for forgiveness, she only thought of how she could get her revenge against Elijah.

Meanwhile, Elijah had gone right up to the top of the mountain and he waited there until God *did* send the rain again. How grateful the people must have been as they saw the first drops of rain, which grew heavier and heavier until at last the dry earth was moist again and everyone could drink as much as they wanted. They knew, too, that soon there would be plenty to eat.

For Elijah it was a wonderful moment. It had not been easy for him to trust God all by himself when all those other prophets were on Baal's side. But now that the people had turned to worship God again and God had shown just how wonderful and powerful he was, Elijah was very, very glad that he had remained loyal to his God.

When the Cock Crowed

Peter lived in a country called Judea, right beside a very big lake. It was such a big lake that it really seemed more like the sea, and so they called it a sea – the Sea of Galilee. Peter used to love to run along the shore with his brother Andrew and then stop to watch the fishermen. They watched them landing the catch of fish or mending the nets. The fishermen always seemed to be busy and Peter thought what an exciting life they must have. He knew that they had to be brave and strong because sometimes terrible storms could blow up on the sea and then you had to fight with every muscle in your body to keep the boat from capsizing. The two brothers looked longingly at the boats. They looked forward very much to the day when they too would be old enough to be fishermen.

But Peter didn't spend all his time on the shore. The hills were nearby and often he used to go to play there, sometimes with Andrew, and sometimes with his friend John.

Of course, they couldn't play all the time. They had to work hard too. Peter and John were Jewish boys and so every morning, except for the Sabbath, they would go along to school. There they would sit on the floor and learn about the Jewish law from their teacher, the Rabbi. They even learned to say lots of passages from the scriptures off by heart.

As he grew older, Peter learnt that his country, Judea, was being ruled, not by his own people, the Jews, but by the Romans who had conquered the land. It made him unhappy and angry to think that his father had to pay taxes to these foreign rulers and that you could get into a lot of trouble if you did not obey them.

One of the things that he had learnt at school was that God had promised the Jews that he would one day send them a Messiah. This Messiah, whoever he might be, was going to set the people free. It actually said in the scriptures that this was going to happen.

Of course, it wasn't always easy to understand just exactly what the scriptures meant and it didn't say *when* this Messiah was going to come, but Peter used to think about it a lot. It would be marvellous if the Messiah could raise an army and fight against the Romans and defeat them! The Jewish people would then be free to have their own leaders once again.

When Peter grew up, he and Andrew did become fishermen. They found they didn't have as much time for studying and thinking as they had when they were boys. Peter's friend, John, was also a fisherman and they used to help one another when they were particularly busy.

Peter got married and settled down happily with his new wife. It *was* hard work being a fisherman, just as he'd known it would be, but he didn't mind too much because he loved his job. Life went on very peacefully in the little village by the sea.

Then some rumours began to spread around the village. There was a man called John going round the countryside. He was telling people that they must ask God to forgive them for the wrong things they had done, because the time was coming when God would rule the world. Crowds of people gathered to hear what John had to say. He could have been quite a hero, but he always reminded people that they should not bother too much about him, because soon someone else was going to come who would be far more important. This was the person the Jewish people had been eagerly awaiting for thousands of years – the Messiah.

Peter's brother, Andrew, was very excited about what John had to say. He would go and listen to him preaching whenever he could. One day Peter had stayed at home whilst Andrew went off to hear John again.

'I wonder what he'll have to tell us when he comes home this time,' thought Peter. He didn't have to wait long to find out.

A breathless Andrew rushed into the house and grabbed his brother. 'You've got to come, Peter,' he panted, 'he's here, the Messiah. John pointed him out to us and we've been talking to him.'

Peter did not need to be told twice. He ran after Andrew and they made their way back to the place where Jesus was staying.

It was strange, thought Peter. Jesus didn't look like a King. He was wearing the same sort of clothes as any ordinary man. But there was something about him, a magnetism that drew Peter to him. He knew that Jesus was no ordinary man. The two brothers stayed with Jesus and listened to him preaching. Great crowds were coming to hear him.

When Jesus asked them if they would be among the small group of men who would help him in his work, they knew at once what they would say. Even if it meant leaving their families for weeks at a time, and leaving their jobs as fishermen, they knew they must go with Jesus. Peter was very glad when Jesus also chose his old friend, John, to be amongst the group of twelve men. They were called 'disciples' because that meant that they were learners and, before they could really help Jesus, they had to learn from him.

The life he was living now was more exciting than anything Peter had ever known. Everywhere they went Jesus would stop and preach and he would also heal people who were suffering from the most terrible diseases. He was able to make blind people see again, and deaf people hear. People who had been crippled were able to walk normally again. No wonder crowds of people turned out every time Jesus and his disciples were in the area.

One day Jesus took the disciples up on to a mountain and spent a long time teaching them there. Peter could hardly take it in because Jesus was saying such amazing and wonderful things. Somehow he seemed to be saying that, if you were his follower, you could actually *be* good from inside.

As the weeks went by and Peter and the other disciples travelled around with Jesus and saw what amazing things he could do, Peter knew that he wanted to follow Jesus and be loyal to him always. Then the day came when Jesus told the disciples that he wanted them to go out and preach and teach and heal people themselves.

They went in twos, travelling round from town to town. Although many people welcomed them and were very happy to turn from their wrong ways and follow Jesus, some people didn't like what Peter and his friend were saying. Often people were unkind to them, but the tremendous thing was that Peter knew that Jesus had given him the power to preach, to heal, and to keep going, even though he was very tired, and that made all the difference.

Peter had thought a lot since he became a follower of Jesus. He remembered what he had learnt at school about the Messiah who was going to set the Jewish people free. But although Jesus was very popular and large crowds gathered wherever he went, there was never any talk of turning these crowds of people into an army. Somehow Peter did not think that Jesus had any plans to lead a rebellion against the Roman occupying forces.

When Peter realised this he was disappointed. But, at the same time, he could not be completely dejected because he began to think of all the things that Jesus *had* done, and the power he had. He had power to heal people, even power to make people come alive who had been dead, and the power to forgive sins. As he thought, things began to click into place and so, when Jesus asked the disciples a rather unusual question, Peter knew at once what he would answer.

They were all sitting down having a rest one day when Jesus said, 'Who are men saying that I am?' The disciples had plenty of answers to that question.

'Some say that you are John, the man who warned people that you were coming; some say that you are Elijah or Jeremiah or one of the other prophets.'

'But who do *you* say I am?' asked Jesus.'

'You are the Messiah, the son of the living God,' said Peter. Jesus turned to speak to him. 'God has blessed you, Peter,' he said, 'because he has shown you this.'

Jesus was the Messiah. He was not the sort of Messiah Peter had expected, but if God had chosen to send his son to free the Jewish people, then things were sure to work out right in the end. Peter's heart gave a jump. He felt happy and hopeful. Then his happiness was shattered. Jesus was talking a different way now. Jesus was actually saying that he was going to be put to death. The Messiah, put to death! How could he talk this way?

Several weeks passed by. It was getting near to the time of the Feast of the Passover. This was a big Jewish festival celebrated every year and thousands of Jews would flock into the capital city, Jerusalem, for the feast.

Jesus sent Peter and John ahead to get a room ready where they could all have the feast together. They arranged a table with the thirteen low couches around it on which they would sit. The food was prepared. There was specially baked bread, wine, water and herbs, and on a side table was a big plate of roast lamb. The lamps that hung down from the ceiling were lit. Everything was ready.

It was a strangely wonderful meal. To be together like that was marvellous; yet it was as if there was a black cloud hanging over them. Jesus had said he was going to die.

'One of you here is going to betray me,' he said.

A murmur of horror spread around the group. 'Is it me?' 'Is it me?' they all said. Judas asked the question too but he already knew the answer, and so did Jesus. Nervously Judas felt the thirty silver coins in his money bag, the bribe money the chief priests had given him to betray Jesus.

Jesus then took the bread and wine from the table and gave it to them to eat and drink. Peter felt so close to Jesus at that moment. He would do anything for him, go anywhere with him.

After the meal Judas slipped away, and the others all went out on to a nearby hill. The grass was soft and green and there were olive trees growing. People who were staying in Jerusalem for the feast had pitched their tents on the side of the hill. It was a beautiful sight in the moonlight.

But Peter was unhappy. He looked at Jesus, who seemed so tired, so worn, as if he were carrying all the cares of the world on his shoulders. Still Peter was not prepared for what Jesus was about to say. 'Tonight you are all going to desert me.' Peter was so shocked he did not wait to hear what Jesus said next.

'Even if everyone else deserts you I won't,' he blurted out.

But Jesus continued, 'Before the cock crows at

dawn you will deny me three times.'

Deny Jesus! It was impossible. 'I would die first,' he insisted.

That night was like a nightmare. Peter had not known that it was possible to be so tired, so worried, so disappointed and unhappy all at the same time. Jesus had taken Peter and two of the other disciples with him into a garden to pray but they had not even been able to do that. Twice Jesus had come and found them asleep!

Then, as they left the garden, the crowd arrived. Soldiers with swords took Jesus and arrested him. Peter panicked. He grabbed a sword from the servant of one of the Jewish leaders and, wielding it, cut off his ear. Jesus did not fight. More and more people arrived on the scene. There seemed to be soldiers everywhere with angry men shouting and waving clubs in their hands. Peter looked around. The other disciples had disappeared. His heart pounding, he fled too.

Peter got his breath back. What should he do? He could not just leave Jesus without seeing what was going to happen to him. Keeping well to the back, he followed the crowd as they took Jesus to the home of Caiaphas, the chief of the Jewish leaders. He sat in the courtyard with some of the soldiers and waited. Inside there was a lot of noise. Many of the Jewish leaders were there. It seemed that they were trying to make a case against Jesus. People were being bribed to tell lies about him. Still nothing happened. Peter shuffled nervously as he waited outside. Suddenly there was a great commotion inside. There were loud shouts of 'Death! Death!'

Just then a girl came up to Peter. She had overheard him speaking and recognised his Galilean accent.

'You were with Jesus, weren't you?' she said.

Cold panic struck Peter. What if they should arrest him too, even put him to death? He turned angrily to the girl. 'I don't even know what you are talking about,' he snapped.

Peter got up and made his way towards the gate. This was no place for him now. But by the gate another girl pointed to him and he heard her say, 'This man was with Jesus.'

'I don't even know the man,' he retorted, trying to sound convincing. He took another step towards the gate but he wasn't going to get away so easily.

A group of men came over to him. 'You must be one of his disciples,' they insisted, 'we can tell by your accent.'

Peter then lost his temper. He cursed and swore at the men, shouting that he didn't even know Jesus.

A shrill sound pierced the early morning air. Peter stopped. Then he recognised that sound. It was the crow of the cockerel. His mind filled with the memory of what Jesus had said to him the night before, 'Before the cock crows........' He'd done it! He'd denied Jesus. He, Peter, the one who was always going to be loyal, had denied Jesus.

Pushing through the crowd of men, he ran out of the courtyard. He ran and ran and ran. Then, when he could run no more, Peter, a grown man, sat down and cried.

A New Kind of Power

Peter was very miserable. It seemed that every-thing had gone as wrong as it could go. The Roman soldiers had killed Jesus. They had hung him on a big wooden cross and left him to die. Now some of his friends had taken his body, wrapped it in long strips of cloth, and put him in a tomb, a cave in the hillside.

Something else had happened. It made Peter feel sick even to think about it. But, somehow, he just could not get it out of his mind. He had denied that he knew Jesus. When he could have defended him, stayed with him right to the end, he had taken the coward's way out.

It helped a little bit to talk to his friend John. Of course John could not approve of what Peter had done, but at least he understood. He knew how frightened they had all been on that terrible night, only the Thursday before, when Jesus was arrested. What Peter longed to do was to talk to Jesus himself, just to say he was sorry. But that was impossible now. Jesus was dead.

All day Saturday Peter moped around the house. He was staying with John, and Mary, Jesus' mother was there too. He was pleased that he was not alone. There was just a little bit of comfort in being able to share his sadness with other people. Wearily they went to bed that night. Peter could hear muffled sobs coming from Mary's bed. The lamp was put out and, as he lay in the darkness, Peter felt that blackness had come right inside him. Gradually tiredness engulfed him and he fell asleep.

Bang, bang, clatter! Peter woke with a start. What was that noise? He blinked and rubbed his eyes. Sunlight was streaming in through the window. Was it really morning already? The banging continued. There was someone at the door. Hurriedly Peter put on his clothes and went to investigate.

There on the doorstep was Mary Magdalene, an old friend of theirs and, also, a follower of Jesus. She was breathless from running, and tears were streaming down her face. John was up by this time and between them they tried to calm her down.

Mary could only blurt out 'They've taken away Jesus' body out of the tomb.'

Jesus' body stolen! This seemed like the final straw. Leaving Mary in the house, Peter raced to the garden where the tomb was, with John close on his heels.

From a distance they saw the big stone, that had blocked the entrance to the tomb, rolled to one side. They ran nearer and, their hearts pounding, looked in. It was true what Mary had said. Jesus' body wasn't there. Only the strips of cloth he had been wrapped in were there, wrapped just as they had been when the body was inside them.

Slowly Peter and John made their way home. Mary Magdalene had left the house. They talked over what they had seen, but they were mystified when it came to explaining that empty tomb. There was a knock at the door. It was Mary back again. But it wasn't the unhappy, crying Mary they had seen earlier in the morning. She was bubbling over with excitement, her eyes shining with joy. As for what she had to say, it seemed unbelievable. She said she had seen Jesus – alive!

The two men could hardly take it in. Perhaps Mary had just imagined it. But just then some more women arrived. They had seen Jesus too! Peter allowed a tiny flicker of hope to replace some of the blackness inside him. If Jesus was the Son of God, perhaps even this was possible.

Peter's thoughts raced on. His heart leapt. If Jesus was alive then he would be able to talk to him again. Could Jesus ever forgive him for the way he'd let him down? Would he ever trust Peter again and give him a new chance to prove his loyalty?

Peter wondered how he could ever have doubted that Jesus was alive and that he would forgive him. Jesus came to see Peter all by himself, even before he visited the rest of the disciples. He loved Peter. How could he help but forgive him?

Now Peter felt that he could start living again. All the blackness was gone. With four friends he went back to the Sea of Galilee. As he stood by the lake, he thought back to the first time he had met Jesus and left his job as a fisherman to follow him. So much had happened since then.

But he couldn't stand there daydreaming all afternoon.

'I'm going fishing,' he yelled to the others.

What a good idea! It would be good to get out in the boat again. 'We'll come too,' they shouted back. They worked hard that night but they did not catch a single fish. By morning they were tired, hungry and disappointed.

Then someone spotted a man on the beach.

He shouted to them, 'Have you caught any fish?' When they said they hadn't he told them to throw out the net again on the right hand side of the boat. It seemed a silly thing to suggest. If they had not caught any fish all night they were hardly likely to now. Still, perhaps it was worth a try.

It was time to pull in the net, but they simply could not. It was brim full of fish. It was a miracle. That man on the shore, who was he?

'It's the Lord!' exclaimed John to Peter. Peter jumped into the water and swam ashore. What a morning it was. They had breakfast of bread and cooked fish together on the beach. After that Jesus had something important to say to Peter.

Once he was sure that Peter really loved him, Jesus knew that he could count on his loyalty. He was putting Peter in a very responsible position. He wanted him to look after other Christians and to help them as much as he could. It was wonderful for Peter to know that Jesus trusted him completely.

All the disciples made their way back to Jerusalem. Jesus told them to wait there because he was going to send his Holy Spirit to be with them. They did not really understand what this meant, but they soon found out. The time had come for Jesus to go back to live with his Father in Heaven. In amazement they stood and watched as Jesus disappeared into a cloud. Then they saw two angels who told them that one day Jesus would come back to earth again in just the same way as he had gone away.

What an experience! The disciples all felt quite shaken, but they were not sad, as they had been when Jesus was put to death. They felt that something wonderful was about to happen, and so they waited. One day the disciples and the other Christians were meeting to pray together when they heard a noise. What could it be? It was as if there was a tremendous wind howling round the room where they were gathered.

The wind was inside the room now, and then, as the Christians stared in amazement, they saw that there was a little flame of fire burning above everyone's head. Peter suddenly knew that a wonderful new power had come inside him. This must be the Holy Spirit that Jesus had said he would send them.

A crowd of people had gathered outside. They had heard the wind and had come to investigate.

'What is going on?' they asked. Peter stepped out and began to talk to them. Somehow it seemed natural that he should be the one to do the talking. With this new power within him he wasn't ashamed to be loyal to Jesus this time. He told the people how Jesus had been put to death but then how he had come to life again and that he was living in heaven with his Father God.

The big crowd grew silent. The people were listening. This was really something to think about.

'What shall we do?' some of them asked. Peter explained how they had to turn away from the wrong things in their lives and come back to live God's way. That day about three thousand people became Christians, followers of Jesus.

The days that followed were so exciting that Peter could hardly believe what was happening. Each day there were more and more Christians. They shared things, helped each other, had wonderful meals together and prayed together.

One day Peter and John were going into the Temple when they saw a lame man begging for money. They had no money with them, but they wanted to give him something far more precious. Using the name and the power of Jesus, they told the man to get up and walk. And there he was, leaping for joy in the Temple! When the news of what had happened spread around the city a crowd of people gathered to see the man who had been healed. That gave Peter another opportunity to preach to them!

Evening came and Peter and John were still talking to the people when a group of stern faced men approached. There was the Chief Jewish Priest, the Captain of the Temple Police and some other men. They didn't like all this talk about Jesus rising from the dead. They arrested Peter and John and threw them into prison for the night.

The next day they were brought up before the Jewish council.

'Who gave you the authority to heal the lame man?' they were asked.

Peter spoke up bravely. 'We did it in the name and

power of Jesus from Nazareth.'

The Jewish leaders were worried. They didn't know what to do with Peter and John. Eventually they decided just to give them a warning.

'You mustn't speak about Jesus again,' they said. Then they let the two men go.

Not speak about Jesus! It was impossible! Peter knew he couldn't obey an order like that. His first loyalty must be to God and Jesus had told them to speak about him. More and more people became Christians. More and more people were healed. Once again the Jewish council arrested the two preachers. They were put in prison for the night.

In the morning some men from the Temple Police Force went round to the jail. They were going to take Peter and John to the trial. The guards outside opened the heavy gate to let the policemen in. Once inside, the policemen blinked in amazement. They must be imagining things. The prisoners weren't there! But they weren't imagining it, for, during the night an angel had come and helped Peter and John to escape without the guards knowing it.

Already Peter and John were preaching to people in the Temple. The police captain went this time with his men to arrest them. Now they were really in trouble. The Jewish leaders were furious.

'Didn't we tell you never to preach about Jesus?' they demanded.

Peter was frightened but he knew what he must say. 'We must obey God rather than men,' he replied.

The chief priest was white with anger. Peter's heart thumped as the leaders decided what to do.

Now they were talking about putting Peter and John to death. Yes that was it. Or was it?

Just then a man called Gamaliel stepped forward. He was a teacher of the Jewish Law, and everyone respected him. He had something important to say to the leaders, but first Peter and John were led out of earshot.

'You must be careful what you do with these men,' said Gamaliel. 'There have been other men who have had their bands of followers in the past but nothing ever came of them. If these are just men preaching with ordinary human powers then their group will also die out in time. But if God is really with them in what they are doing, then you will not be able to stop them.'

'Yes,' agreed the Jewish leaders. 'There is some sense in what Gamaliel says.'

Peter and John were brought back to the trial. They were not going to be killed after all. But they *were* going to be beaten.

After it was over, the two friends limped away. Peter's back hurt very badly but somehow Peter was not sad. In fact he was very happy. Happy that he had been able to suffer for Jesus, and happy too that this time he had not let Jesus down.

'Curse Christ – and Live'

Life for a slave was not much fun. You had to do exactly what your owner told you. There was little time to play with your friends and you didn't get any pocket-money. But for Polycarp, a boy who came from the land that we now call Turkey, there were some good things as well. His mistress, Callisto, was very kind to him and did not make him work *too* hard. Then there were the wonderful times when John would come and tell them stories. Polycarp had been captured when soldiers of the Roman Empire invaded and conquered his land. He had been very young when they had sold him as a slave.

John, by contrast, was a very old man. He had a long, white beard, and might have looked a bit frightening to Polycarp if it had not been for the twinkle in his eye and the smile that often crossed his face. The stories he had to tell were the most exciting Polycarp had ever heard. For John had been a disciple of Jesus and he loved to talk about the things Jesus had done and the wonderful times Jesus and his disciples had had together.

As he grew up, Polycarp knew that he wanted to be a follower of Jesus too. Even though he could not see him, he knew that Jesus was his friend. He wanted other people to know Jesus too, and he would travel around telling people about Jesus and helping people who were in trouble.

When Callisto died, she left all her money to Polycarp in her will. Now he could live an easy life, in a big house, with all the comforts he wanted. But Polycarp knew that God had plenty of work for him to do. Besides, there were lots of people far poorer than he was. So Polycarp gave away all the money he had been left. He was such a kind, generous person. No wonder the people loved and respected him.

One day news spread amongst the Christians that they were going to have a visitor. Roman soldiers had arrested a man called Ignatius. Now they were marching him for hundreds of miles to take him to Rome and he would pass through Smyrna, where Polycarp lived, on his journey. Poor Ignatius! He was already very old. It was very hard to walk, day after day, over dusty roads with the sun beating down on him. He did not have much to look forward to at the end of the journey either. For, when he got there, the Roman Emperor was going to have him executed.

When the little party reached Smyrna, the soldiers allowed the Christians there to look after Ignatius for a few days. They bathed his cut feet, they gave him the best food and the softest bed. Although he had suffered so much, Ignatius was not downhearted. For Polycarp it was wonderful to meet someone who faced his death so cheerfully. Even after he had started out again on his long journey to Rome, Ignatius wrote letters to Polycarp encouraging him in his work.

Perhaps Polycarp wondered how he would react if he were in Ignatius' shoes. Would he stay loyal to God, even if it meant dying for his faith? Throughout his long life, he carried on with the work of teaching people about Jesus, and he never forgot the advice of Ignatius. But as Polycarp grew older, Nero, the cruel Roman Emperor, died. The new Emperor decided that the persecution of the Christians should stop. No more Christians should be hunted out to be thrown into arenas where big crowds would watch them being attacked and killed by wild animals.

In Smyrna, however, some people were planning to hold games in the local arena. There would be a display of gymnastics and some sword play to begin with. But the organisers knew that it was the spectacle of animals killing human beings that the crowd really loved to watch. The Emperor wouldn't be attending the games so perhaps they could organise some real 'entertainment' without him knowing.

As the organisers made their preparations for the games, Polycarp had a strange and frightening experience. One night in bed he felt that he was getting hotter and hotter. There were flames lapping round his pillow. He was being burnt alive! He woke up with a start. So, it was only a dream after all! But Polycarp felt that it was more than a dream. Perhaps it was a premonition about something that was going to happen to him.

Within a few days the preparations for the games were complete. A group of Christians were arrested and, when the time came, they were herded into the arena. The crowd grew excited as one Christian after another was torn to pieces. They wanted more and more. Then a small group began to think. Who was the teacher of these Christians? Why should he escape?

'Let's have Polycarp,' they began to shout, and soon the chant was coming from the whole crowd: 'Polycarp! Polycarp!'

Sitting in the arena were one or two Christians who had gone unnoticed. It was bad enough seeing their fellow Christians suffering so. It would be terrible if Polycarp, their kind, gentle leader, should also be killed. When no one was looking they slipped out of the arena and hurried to where Polycarp was living.

Panting with fear and exhaustion from running, they arrived at the house. They told Polycarp how their friends had been put to death and that the crowd was now calling for *him* to be thrown to the wild beasts. Polycarp looked calm and thoughtful. He was sure that the dream he had had meant that he was going to be burnt to death. Perhaps his time had come now.

But his young friends persuaded him to move to another house where the Roman soldiers might not find him. Quietly he waited there to see what would happen. Then there was a thud of footsteps coming up the road to the house. The soldiers had tortured a slave boy until he had finally told them where to find Polycarp. As they entered the house, the soldiers were amazed to see the old man they had been sent to arrest.

Polycarp welcomed them. He offered them food and then asked if they would let him pray for an hour. The soldiers looked on in wonder as Polycarp talked to God, not for one, but for two whole hours. They did not want to arrest this kind old man but they had their job to do, and so they escorted him into Smyrna.

As they approached the town, the little group saw an imposing man waiting for them. It was the Chief of Police. He did not want Polycarp to be killed either, so he had come to see if there was any way out of the situation. He invited Polycarp to sit with him in his carriage. He tried to reason with him.

'Surely it isn't so much to say Caesar is Lord,' he said, 'then the whole business will be over and you can go free.'

But Polycarp knew that, if Caesar was Lord, Jesus could never be Lord, too, and he knew to whom his first loyalty must be. He would not agree to the suggestion, and so the Police Chief, having done all he could, drove Polycarp to the arena.

A great cheer went up from the crowd as they saw Polycarp walk into the arena. With his head held high, he walked calmly over to where the Proconsul was sitting. As the Emperor was not at the games, the Proconsul was the most senior member of the Roman government present.

Then, above the noise of the cheering crowd, a voice thundered out, 'Be strong Polycarp and play the man.' Silence fell over the vast arena. Where had the voice come from? The crowd began to murmur; they looked around the arena but they could not see the owner of that thunderous voice. People began to fidget nervously in their seats. Could it be a voice from heaven? The tension broke as the cheering and shouting began again, this time more loudly than before.

The Proconsul was worried. He knew that the Emperor would be angry if he heard that Polycarp had been killed simply because of the crowd's demand. He was a kind man himself and he did not want to see this old man put to death for no good reason. All the same the crowd was angry and impatient by this time. The Proconsul doubted if he could control them if they did not get their own way.

He looked at Polycarp standing in front of him with a steadfast look on his face.

'If you will curse Christ I will let you go,' he said.

But Polycarp knew that was something he could never do. With a steady voice he replied, 'For eighty six years I have served him and he has never done me wrong. How then can I blaspheme my King who saved me?'

Now Polycarp's fate appeared to be sealed. The Proconsul sent a messenger round the arena to give the crowd the news that Polycarp had refused to curse Christ. But there was one more person who wanted to save him. The ruler of the games announced to the crowd that the wild animals had been shut in their cages for the night. According to the rules of the games they could not be let into the arena again that day.

The crowd were now so angry that they decided to take matters into their own hands. They surged

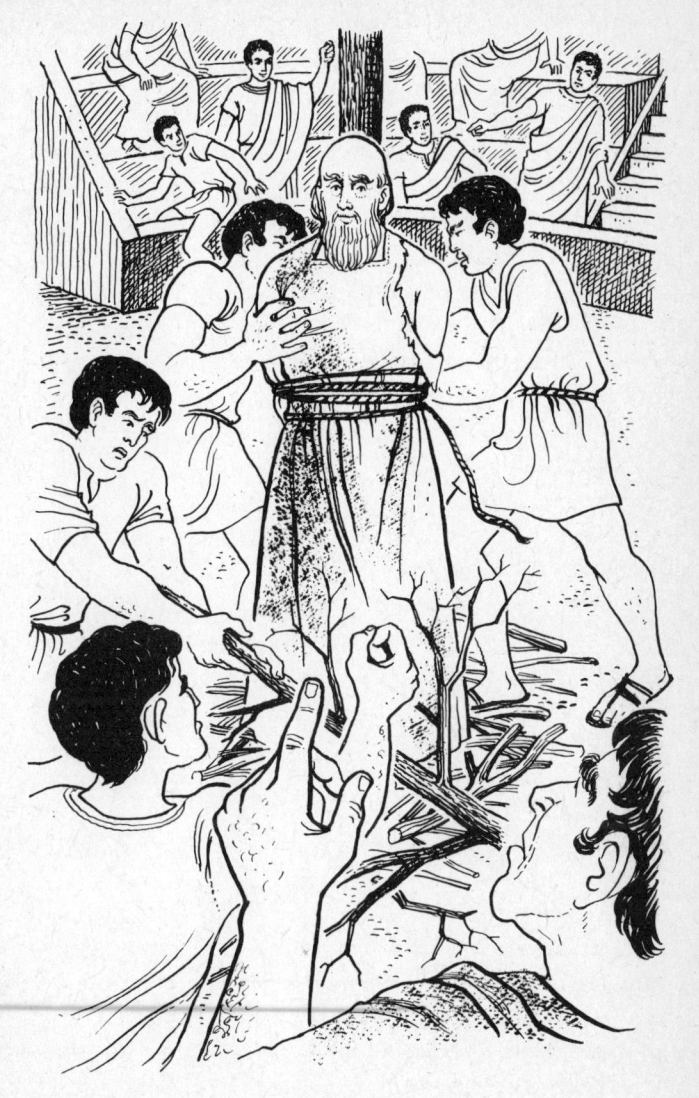

out of their places and went in search of firewood. Then they made a big bonfire in the arena and tied Polycarp to a stake in the middle of it. The firewood was lit and the flames lapped round the stake. But then the crowd looked on in awe as they watched the flames, for they were not touching Polycarp, but burning in a circle around him. His dream of the previous night had come true.

A soldier stepped forward and plunged his sword into Polycarp. And so Polycarp, like Ignatius many years before, was loyal to Jesus even though it led to his death.

The Man from Verulamium

Alban was born in Britain only 300 years after the birth of Christ, but the town he grew up in was one of the largest towns in Britain, with many sturdy stone houses, roofed with big, red tiles.

The town was called Verulamium, and Alban's parents were not Britons, or natives of the British Isles, but Roman citizens. Many years before, the Romans had conquered Britain and now they were ruling the country.

In the middle of Verulamium there was the Forum, a big square surrounded by shops on three sides, with the baths making up the fourth side.

Alban liked to go shopping with his mother. He watched, fascinated, as the butcher weighed out the meat. Then they would peer at the glittering jewelry laid out on the counter of the next shop. The Forum was crowded with shoppers. There were slaves in their short, brown tunics and Britons in their brightly coloured coarse woollen clothes. But the smartest people were certainly the Romans. Alban's mother and the other women wore long, elegant dresses and cloaks whilst the men wore fine white robes called togas.

Mingling with the crowd there were always Roman soldiers. They were so big and strong and Alban thought they looked magnificent in their shining brass helmets, topped with red crests. He longed for the day when he, too, could be a soldier. Of course, Alban and his friends could always play at being soldiers. They would march up and down on the marble floors in his house until his mother, in exasperation, would send them outside to play.

In one room of the house there was a shrine, a table where Alban's parents would burn incense as a sacrifice, or present, to Jupiter, Saturn, Venus or one of the other Roman gods. They thought that this would make the gods pleased with them so that they would be able to live happy, prosperous lives.

As Alban grew older, his parents told him that soon he would be leaving Britain and going to school in Rome. He was nervous at the thought of leaving his family and travelling many hundreds of miles to the big city. But, if you were a Roman boy, you were not allowed to show that you were scared. So Alban put on a brave face. Once he got to Rome, there was so much to do and learn that he hardly had time to feel homesick.

In addition to mathematics and science and other school subjects, Alban learned about the Roman laws. He also learned how to be a good soldier. By the time he was ready to come home to Verulamium he was old enough to be an officer in the Roman army.

Verulamium was an important military centre. Legions of soldiers would set off from there on their long march along the road called Watling Street, all the way to Chester, and even on to York and

Hadrian's Wall. Alban loved his life as a soldier and worked hard to train his men well.

As an army officer, Alban was allowed to have his own house. His kindness, generosity and friendly nature made him a popular young man and he would often invite his friends round to his house. Apart from his friends, he found himself interested in another group of people. These were the Christians. He knew that the authorities did not like them because they refused to offer sacrifices to Caesar, the Roman Emperor. But Alban admired the bravery of the Christians. They were always ready to stand up for what they believed, even when it meant danger, or even death.

One night, Alban heard a knocking at his door. He went to see who it was and saw a young man dressed in a dark cloak. He had obviously been running. When the man had rested, he explained to Alban that he was being followed and that he desperately needed somewhere to spend the night. Alban was not the sort of person to turn away anyone in trouble.

'Come on in,' he said. Then he showed the man to a room where he could hide, and told his servants not to tell anyone about the unexpected guest.

Now Alban could find out who the stranger was. He said that he was a Christian priest. The Roman authorities were hunting him and would probably put him to death if they captured him. Alban listened intently. There was something different about this man. He was so calm. What was it that made him willing to risk his life for his religion?

'I'll let him hide here for as long as he needs until the danger is past,' he thought.

Alban and the priest became good friends. They had long talks together and the priest began to tell Alban about Jesus. An idea formed in Alban's mind. Perhaps he, too, could become a follower of Jesus? He quickly put the thought to one side. He did not want to get himself into trouble. But, as he heard more about Jesus, he realised that to be his follower was the only way of coming to know the one true God. Finally he made up his mind. He wanted to follow Jesus too. He told his friend, the priest, who was thrilled and soon afterwards he baptised Alban as a Christian.

Alban continued to hide his friend but he knew that he was still in danger. So far it had been possible to keep his whereabouts a secret from the authorities. But what if someone should give away the secret? Perhaps one of the servants might accept a bribe to tell where the priest was hiding. It was a possibility Alban and his friend learned to live with. All the same, it came as a shock when Alban looked out of the window one day to see a group of soldiers coming towards the house. They were not men he knew. Alban could think of only one reason for their coming.

The soldiers did the job they had come for. That was a good day's work done now that they had handed the man, dressed in a dark cloak and hood, over to the judge. That was another Christian priest about to be executed. The judge looked at the man before him. Then he looked again. Surely he had seen

him somewhere before.

'Take off your cloak,' he ordered. Then he gasped in recognition. This was no Christian priest but Alban, an officer of the Roman army!

Out of loyalty to his friend, Alban had let him escape. Now he would be punished in his place. At first the judge was embarrassed by the mistake. But when Alban said that he was now a Christian, the judge became angry.

'You must offer sacrifice to Caesar or you will be put to death,' he shouted.

But Alban served the living God now. He could not sacrifice to Caesar. The judge was furious by this time. He ordered men to whip Alban and torture him. Still he refused to sacrifice to the Emperor.

Now the judge carried out his threat. He ordered that Alban should be beheaded. Calmly Alban walked to the room where the block and axe were waiting for him. A soldier was ordered to carry out the execution. He waited for the prisoner to arrive. When he saw Alban's calm, brave face, he felt weak inside. Here was a man who was prepared to die because he had been loyal to the God he believed in and the friend he loved. The soldier faltered. He knew he could not be the one to execute this man.

When the judge heard that the soldier had refused to carry out the execution he was amazed. But his amazement soon turned into even greater anger. 'Let the soldier be executed too,' he ordered. And so Alban and the soldier died together.

After Alban's death, many more people in England became Christians. They wanted to remember the brave man who is said to be the first person in England to have died for his faith in Christ, and so they changed the name of Verulamium to the name it is known by today – St. Albans.

Adventure in China

Far away on the other side of the world is the beautiful country of China. It was there, in a marvellous city by the sea, that Betty had her home. It might seem strange to you that Betty, a little American girl, should live in China, but it didn't seem strange to Betty. Her parents were missionaries. When Betty was still very young they had left America and come to China to tell people about God and his son, Jesus.

Life was very exciting for Betty and her brothers and sisters. They lived near the sea shore and nearly every day they would go and explore in the rock pools, play on the beach and swim in the warm sea. They had lessons, not in a classroom, but at home in a study that opened out on to the garden.

Betty enjoyed being at home with her family and having lessons in her own back garden, but it was never quite the same as going to school. When she was old enough her parents decided to send her to boarding school near the great city of Peking. As she packed her trunk and prepared for the long journey Betty was a little bit nervous. She wondered what school would be like. But she need not have worried. She soon made many friends and enjoyed learning and playing with them.

Betty's friends at school were foreigners as she was, but she also grew to know and love the Chinese people. She came to love God, too, and as she grew older she thought that one day she would become a missionary like her parents, so that she could tell these wonderful people about God who loved them.

But first, Betty had to leave China. It was time for her to go back to America to begin college. What a change from China to America! In China there had always been plenty to do, but here there seemed to be so many *new* things. There were new gadgets: washing machines, carpet sweepers and others that Betty had never seen before. Everywhere people were driving around in fast cars. They always seemed to be in such a hurry!

Life at college was certainly different from the sheltered home in China, but Betty enjoyed it. She worked hard at her lessons and she made friends. Like all girls, Betty would sometimes daydream about the man she would marry. He would be tall and handsome, friendly and full of fun. He would be a Christian, someone who had given his life to Jesus to live for him.

When the time came for her to leave college, Betty was more sure than ever that she wanted to go back to China as a missionary. She knew that she would need to know as much as she could about the Bible and she wanted to learn more about how to share her faith in Jesus with other people. So she applied to go to the famous American Christian college called the Moody Bible Institute.

A year after Betty first went to this college,

another young student arrived. His name was John Stam. John had grown up in a small American town, in a simple wooden house that his father had built. As he had five brothers he never lacked anyone to play with and he loved the games of baseball and the many adventures they had.

John's parents were Christians. His father had started a mission in the town and there many people heard about Jesus. When he was fifteen John went along to one of the meetings. He had been many times before but, somehow, this meeting was different. As the speaker talked, John realised how sinful he was and how impossible it was for him to live a good life without Jesus. Soon afterwards he gave his life over to Jesus, to use as he wanted.

Now John was busier than ever. He began to help in the work of the mission. He even started to preach to the people on the streets. After he left school John trained as a business man and then worked in several different offices. As he walked along the street on his way to work he would study the crowds of people passing by. Many of those people did not know Jesus. Slowly John became more and more sure that he must leave his office job and spend his time telling people about Jesus. And so he, too, started to study at the Moody Bible Institute.

From time to time missionaries, home from abroad, would come and speak to the students. John was very interested in what they had to say. Letters also came from missionaries in all corners of the world and John read many of these. A new idea came to him. 'Could God want me to go abroad as a missionary?' he wondered. He was attracted to the land of China. It was so big. There were so many millions of people there who had never heard of Jesus.

As he grew more interested in China, John began to go to special meetings where people prayed for the work of the missionaries who were already working in that distant land. There was someone else who also attended those meetings. John could not help noticing the girl with the long, dark hair and lovely gentle face. They got to know each other and soon John and Betty had fallen in love. They would have liked to marry right away, but they knew there were reasons why they should not.

Betty was in her last term at college. She was all ready to go back to China where she knew God wanted her to work. John was not yet completely sure that God wanted him in China. He still had another year of study and he had to pass a strict medical examination. John and Betty prayed together. They knew that they must put God first and that their first loyalty must be to him. Betty knew it would not be right for her to wait behind in America for John. If God wanted them to marry, then he would bring John to China too.

So Betty set off alone on the long voyage to China. Soon she was busy with the hard job of learning Chinese. How pleased she was that she had lived in China before and the little bit of the language she had once learnt began to come back to her. But, whilst her language studies went well, other things seemed to be going wrong. There were bandits in the part of China where she should have been going to work. Already they had captured one of the missionaries and carried him off into the mountains. Betty had to stay in a safer area until the danger was past.

Two missionaries, Dr. and Mrs Scott, were returning to China after a spell at home. It was a welcome break for Betty to go to meet them at the port of Shanghai. But even there things still seemed to go wrong for Betty. Her throat felt so sore! The pain was still there after a few days and so Betty saw the doctor.

'You must stay here and have those tonsils dealt with,' he told her.

And so poor Betty had to stay in Shanghai for three weeks. Would she ever begin the work she had come to China to do?

But whilst things seemed to be going wrong for Betty, God had been at work. Soon she was to have a wonderful surprise. Another boat was sailing towards Shanghai harbour, a boat from America, and on board was John. Betty and John could hardly believe that they should meet up in Shanghai like this. Now they could get engaged and begin to make plans for their wedding. They had put loyalty to God first and he had given them what they both wanted so much.

What a wedding it was! Betty could hardly believe it was true.

'Here I am,' she thought, 'in the country I love and marrying the man of my dreams. Isn't God good!'

After their honeymoon, John and Betty settled down happily to their work. There was so much to do. John would speak about Jesus at meetings held in the market place and Betty would talk to those who stopped to listen. They would sell parts of the Bible written in Chinese and give away little leaflets telling people how they could become Christians.

Sometimes they had to travel far from home as there were many scattered villages and they wanted to meet the people living in these villages as well as those in the big towns. The roads were often steep and stony. Betty did not know which was the most frightening, to stop and slide down the hill herself, or to be carried in a sort of basket chair by Chinese coolies!

The time soon came, however, when Betty could no longer join John on his trips to the hills, for she was expecting a baby. Soon she knew how wonderful it was to hold baby Helen in her arms and John was as proud and pleased as any father could be.

Betty brought her baby home from hospital, but she knew that soon it would be time for the little family to pack their bags once again. The missionary society had appointed John and Betty to go to Tsingteh, a town far away. There they would be able to tell many people for the first time the good news of Jesus. It was an exciting prospect, but John and Betty knew that there might also be dangers. They had heard rumours about large groups of soldiers coming into the area. The soldiers ate the crops of rice and so the local people went even hungrier than usual. There was also a possibility that fighting might break out and John grew worried. Did God really want him to take his wife and daughter into a place like this? He prayed that God would really show them what they should do.

The most sensible thing would be to find out if the rumours were true. So John and another man went to Tsingteh to see for themselves. The town seemed peaceful enough and even the magistrate said it would be safe for John to bring his family there. On the other hand, some men had been stealing corn and there had been bandits not far away.

When he got home John told Betty what he had found out. Although it seemed fairly safe to go to Tsingteh they could not be certain. They spent a long time talking and praying about their decision. They loved the Chinese people. They longed to tell more of them about Jesus. Eventually they decided that, even if there was danger ahead of them, they must loyally carry out the job God had given them.

And so Betty and John settled down in Tsingteh. They bought a big stove to keep them warm during the winter, for the town was high up in the mountains and the snow lay deep outside.

One morning Betty was busy bathing baby Helen. There was a knock at the door. Who could that be? Betty went to investigate. On the doorstep was a messenger boy. He was out of breath from running and very upset.

'Soldiers have come into the town,' he panted. 'It's not safe to stay here, you must try to leave.'

Betty's heart beat faster but she tried to keep calm. She and John, the cook and the servant girl, all knelt

down on the floor and prayed. Whilst they were still praying, there was another rough knock at the door. This time it was the soldiers. In they came and soon they arrested John and took him away. 'What can they be doing to him?' wondered Betty. But she did not have to wait long to find out, for soon the soldiers were back again. This time they took Betty and the baby.

The next few days were like a bad dream. The soldiers marched the little family over the mountains to another town. John and Betty were tired and hungry, but they knew that God was with them and that helped them. When they reached their destination the guards put them in a house and kept them there for the night. John and Betty did not know what was in store for them, but they were not afraid to die because they knew that then they would be with God in Heaven.

The next morning the soldiers came for them. Betty lay Helen on the bed, snug in her sleeping bag, and she and John went with the soldiers. The soldiers took them up a hill to a clearing in the pine trees. Then a big silver sword flashed in the sky as a soldier beheaded first John and then Betty.

It seemed such a sad end for the young couple. But they had always put God first and he was in control. People back in America heard about the deaths. 'Here are two young people who have been loyal to God, even though it meant going to a country where there were many dangers. They have even died serving God,' they thought. 'We want to be loyal to God, too, whatever the cost.'

What happened to baby Helen? A Christian man found her in the house where her mother had left her. He hid her in a basket and carried her over the mountains. She grew up in her grandparents' home and, when she was old enough, she also worked as a missionary in China, telling people the good news of God's love.

War Cry in the Jungle

Right in the middle of the huge African continent there is a little village called Bopepe. The people there live a very simple, peaceful life. The children go to school just like children all over the world. If you are ill you can go to the clinic and the nurse will be able to help you. On Sundays you can go to worship God in church.

But Bopepe hasn't always been peaceful and happy. There was a time when great trouble came and life was very difficult, especially for Bo Martin, the pastor of a number of village churches.

Bo lived with his wife and children in a house made of a mixture of straw and mud, baked hard in the hot sun. He loved the people in the village, and he worked hard at his job of preaching to them and teaching them how they should live as Christians.

He had also grown to love the two foreign missionaries who had come to live in Bopepe. He was full of admiration for the way they had left their homes to come to help to teach the people about Jesus. Margaret also looked after the people when they were ill, and Mary was a teacher.

Margaret, who had come from England to work in Bopepe, was very tired. There was always so much work to do, so many sick people to see at the little clinic. She liked her work but, all the same, the time had come when she needed a holiday.

Her friends persuaded her to go away for a month's rest. Besides, whilst she was away, she would be able to collect the stores that they badly needed at the little mission station in Bopepe. Bandages, medicines and many more supplies all had to be collected from Stanleyville, a big town almost a hundred miles away from the village.

So Margaret set off on her long journey in a rickety bus over bumpy African roads. Bo and many other people from the village came to wave 'Good bye'. They looked forward to seeing her arrive back in Bopepe after her holiday.

Soon after Margaret left, rumours began to spread around the village. Soldiers had started fighting in other parts of the country and now the Simbas were getting near to Bopepe. The Simbas were soldiers who hated the rulers of the country and wanted to be in charge themselves. They were fighting against the national army.

People were terrified of the Simbas. They knew how cruel they could be. Why, it was said that they would beat people and even kill them for no reason at all. What was more, they hated foreigners and that meant that Bo's friends, the missionaries, would be in great danger.

Mary was left by herself now that Margaret was on holiday. One day she was resting in the afternoon when she heard a noise outside. She sat up. Her heart began to race as she heard voices and footsteps approaching the house. She looked out and saw eight men. They had fur on their hats and around their wrists. These were charms which were supposed to keep them from dying. In their hands they carried rifles. These men were Simbas.

Bo had heard the roar of the engine as the big car screeched to a halt in the village. Then the news reached him that Simbas had gone to Mary's house. What should he do? Bo knew that, if he stood by his fellow Christians, the foreign missionaries, then the Simbas would turn against him. But he knew that, whatever happened, he had to do all he could to help them.

He raced up to the house and heard the commotion inside. The men were shouting and swearing at Mary.

'Let me in,' he cried.

But the door was shut and guarded by a grim faced Simba pointing a rifle.

Eventually they brought Mary on to the verandah.

She looked pale but not afraid as she held her head up and said, 'Go ahead and shoot me.'

The Simba pointed a gun at her head. Bo held his breath, but then the Simba put down his gun. There wasn't much point in killing a woman who was not afraid to die.

The Simbas left the village and Bo and Mary and the other villagers breathed sighs of relief. But that was not the last they would see of the cruel rebel soldiers.

Not long after the Simbas' visit another car arrived in the village. It was one Sunday morning whilst the church service was in progress. A woman jumped out of the passenger seat and ran towards the church, her heart thumping with excitement. It was Margaret back from her holidays! Bo had to bring the service to an end because the people were so thrilled to see her safely back that they were longing to greet her.

Life in Bopepe carried on, but not quite normally. The Simbas would visit the village from time to time and frighten everybody. Mary was not allowed to teach the schoolchildren as she used to do. Bo got into trouble for preaching in church. It became too dangerous for Bo, Margaret, Mary and the other Christians ever to meet together to pray.

Then one night the Simbas arrived again. This time they had not just come to frighten people. They went to see Margaret and Mary and told them, 'You're under arrest.' They had come to take the two missionaries to a town called Banalia which was fifteen miles from Bopepe. Two of the Simbas went to Bo's house. He was arrested also. Now his loyalty to his Christian friends had really landed him in trouble! They took him back to the missionaries' house and they all spent the night there.

The next morning everyone prepared for the journey to Banalia. Margaret and Mary packed their cases. The Simbas let Bo go back to his house for a few minutes to say goodbye to his wife. Then they waited to see if a truck would arrive. 10 o'clock came and still no truck had arrived. The prisoners' hearts sank. That meant they would have to walk. Fifteen miles along dusty roads with the hot sun beating down on them!

The nightmare journey came to an end at last. The three prisoners were pushed into a big house. It had once been a beautiful place, but now it was filthy and almost empty. The Simbas told Bo he was free to go now that Margaret and Mary were safely in Banalia. But Bo wasn't going to walk out and leave his friends in a place like this! Why, there was not even a mattress to sleep on! He went off to see what could be done and found two Simba army officers and another man who was supposed to be in charge of the house.

They brought in an old bedstead and a mattress to go on it, but the mattress only covered a third of the bed. This was no good.

'How do you expect two women to sleep in a place like this?' demanded Bo.

The officers began to get angry. They did not like people who argued with them.

Bo was soon under arrest again. The Simbas made him run right round the town with a spear pointing at his back. Then they locked him up in a dark, damp cell. In that lonely cell Bo prayed for a long time. He knew that he had done the right thing when he had protected Margaret and Mary, but it seemed to be getting him into more and more trouble. He was worried, too, about his wife and children at home in Bopepe. But when he talked to God about it he felt better. He rolled his jacket up to make a pillow, lay down on the stone floor, and was soon asleep.

Several days passed and Bo was still a prisoner. Then, one day, a soldier came and told him he was being released. Mary had pleaded with the Simbas

to let him go and now he was free! It was so good to get back to Bopepe to the people he loved. But it made him sad to think of his missionary friends still under arrest in Banalia.

Mary never came back to Bopepe. There was a lot of fighting between the Simbas and the National Army and gradually the National Army began to win the war. When the news came through that they had once again taken over Stanleyville, the capital, the Simbas were furious. The order was given. All white people must be killed. Angry soldiers burst into the house where the prisoners were being held in Banalia. They marched the little group of people, men, women and children, down to the river and then shot them, one by one. Mary, the woman who was not afraid to die, was one of those people.

But what had happened to Margaret? Only a few days before her friends were killed, the Simbas had allowed her to return to Bopepe. Bo was thrilled to see her back in the village, but he knew how dangerous it was for her there. She had to go into hiding in the jungle and there Bo looked after her. He brought her food and built her a shelter. Margaret was so thankful for her loyal friend, but she knew what a risk he was running in hiding her. If the Simbas found out, not only Bo, but all the villagers might be killed.

Bo was captured and sentenced to death. Three times he was taken to the place of execution, three times the officer-in-charge could not give the order to shoot. He had had a dream in which he stood before God and God told him that if he shot Bo he, the officer would die. After the third attempt he told Bo of his dream and gave him a free pardon and a road pass.

So Margaret said goodbye to Bo. All he could do now was to pray for her, until at last, many months later, he heard good news. Margaret had been rescued by soldiers in the National Army. She was safe at home in England.

Bo was at the airport to greet Margaret on the return to Congo, two years later.

From then on things were better. The Simbas quickly lost ground and soon the National Army was once more in control. Bo and the other villagers could start to build their village again. Houses were erected, and a new school and church. In the village Bo was able to carry on with his work as pastor and new missionaries arrived to help with the work. There was so much to do, now that everything could begin again. Bo never forgot his friends, Margaret and Mary. They were not in Bopepe any longer, but he often thought about the good times and the hard times they had had together. He was glad now that he had been loyal to them, even in those hard times.

Prison Sentence

In 1941 Russia was at war. Hundreds of people were suffering and dying each day; there was not enough food to go round and many houses were in ruins. It was during these hard times that Aida Skripnikova was born. Her home was in the big Russian city called Leningrad.

In spite of the war, Aida and her brother and sister had plenty of fun together. When it was unsafe to play in the streets they would stay indoors and peep out through the windows at the passing world. Often they would see soldiers marching past but Aida never saw her own father marching with the soldiers. He did not believe in killing other people and so he would not join the army. When Aida was just a baby, soldiers had taken her father away and shot him because of his beliefs.

It was hard for Mrs. Skripnikova to bring up three children without a husband to help her but she did her best. She tried to teach them to live as God wanted them to live and, when the day's work was finished, she would tell them stories about Jesus.

When Aida was four years old the war came to an end. Times were still hard, but gradually there was more food for the little family and warmer clothes to keep out the cold winter winds. Aida liked school.

There was so much to learn, and so many friends to play with. But, as she grew older, Aida became puzzled. Many of her friends said they didn't believe in God. Aida's mother had always taught her that God was there looking after her.

Then one day her brother started talking about Jesus. 'I've come to know Jesus for myself,' he said. 'I've given my life to him.'

Aida worshipped her older brother. She thought, 'If he can talk like this, then there must be something in it.'

For many weeks Aida thought about what her brother had said. She decided that, if God really *was* there and it was possible to know him, then this was what she wanted. One Sunday she decided to go to church. It was unusual for a teenager to go to church. Her friends would probably laugh at her if they knew she was going. But Aida enjoyed the service. The people there really loved God. They seemed certain that he would help them and that, even when they died, they would still be with him. After the service Aida met an English boy. He was a Christian, too. She asked him a lot of questions about his faith in Jesus. Over the next few weeks he and other people from the church helped her a lot. They explained how God wanted to forgive all the wrong things she had done, and how Jesus would be her friend and help her to live God's way if she would only give her life to him. Of course, it wouldn't be an easy life, Aida knew that. But, as soon as she had given her life to God, she felt happier than she'd ever felt and she knew that he was really with her.

About this time,* something very sad happened. Aida's brother died. She missed him very much. The house seemed so empty without the sound of his cheerful whistling and laughing voice. But, as Aida talked to God, she knew that he understood. Somehow that made all the difference and she began to feel better.

Now that she was a Christian, Aida found that her life was changing. She spent time reading her Bible and meeting with other Christians to worship the God they all loved. She had already left school and was working in a science laboratory. It was interesting work and Aida had made friends there. As she got to know them, she realised that they weren't as happy with life as she was because they didn't know God. In fact, every day she must pass hundreds of people on the streets who didn't know God either. Aida felt desperately sorry for them. 'What can I do to help them?' she wondered.

Then Aida had an idea. 'I know', she thought, 'I'll write a poem telling people about God and how important it is that they should become his friends.' So she wrote the poem and then copied it out on to postcards in her best handwriting.

Soon it would be New Year's Eve. 'I'll give out the postcards on that day,' she decided. 'It will be my way of wishing people a happy New Year.' So Aida wrapped herself up as warmly as she could and, standing on a street corner in the middle of Lenin-

* It is not clear whether Aida's brother died before or after she became a Christian.

grad, handed out copies of her poem to the passers-by as they hurried home from work on that cold December evening.

A few weeks later Aida was at home. Tap.. Tap... Who would that be at the door? She went to investigate. As she opened the door her heart missed a beat. There on the step was a stern-faced policeman. 'Are you Aida Skripnikova?', he asked. Aida grew pale as he told her that he had come to arrest her. She would be brought to trial for giving out religious literature. The Russian authorities did not want people to believe in God. Since Aida had tried to tell other people about him, they would punish her.

Aida was only 20 years old. After the trial, she had to leave her job in the laboratory and go to work on a building site. It was hard work. Her hands were soon rough with digging and carrying stones. Then there were other things that made life hard. People were unkind to her and often made fun of her. There were even articles written in newspapers criticising her and her belief in Jesus. Finally, Aida received a letter saying that she could no longer live in Leningrad. She would have to move away from all her friends to another town.

Of course, Aida was upset. But she knew that, if these hard things happened to her because she was loyal to God, he would help her to live through them. Many of her friends though did not know God yet. It would be difficult for them to understand why she was willing to go through so much hardship for him. Aida longed to explain to them. It would take too long to write a letter to each of them, so Aida decided that she would write an article explaining her Christian faith. She would have copies of it printed so that she could send a copy to each friend. Her friends were interested in the article. Some of them decided to print more copies, and so more people were able to read about God and his Son, Jesus.

Aida was not the only person to be persecuted for her faith. Many other Christians were going through hard times. Some were in prison, some had even died. Sometimes the authorities would take away children from their Christian parents.

Aida thought, 'If I could tell people in other countries what is happening, then perhaps the Russian authorities would be kinder to the Christians here.' It was difficult to meet foreigners who visited Russia but Aida managed to see some of them in secret. When the foreigners returned home they told what they had learnt about the Russian Christians.

What a busy life Aida had! She was working during the day; meeting her Christian friends and meeting foreign visitors whenever she could. In addition to all this, she was helping to get copies of two magazines to as many people as possible. These magazines spoke of the love and the power of God. Whilst she was so busy, Aida knew how important it is to talk to God in prayer. The authorities did not allow Christians to meet together to pray and so Aida and her friends had a secret meeting place in the woods.

One night the little group was meeting in the

woodland clearing. It was bitterly cold, but they scarcely noticed the freezing temperature because they were so happy to be talking to God. Suddenly they heard a sound in the distance. Men were crashing their way through the undergrowth, heading in their direction. There was a dazzle of torchlight as the police swooped in on the group. Some people ran away but Aida was trapped. A policeman grabbed at her roughly, pulling her hair. She was under arrest for a second time.

The trial was like a nightmare. It was not held in a courtroom, but in a local factory. From all around people were shouting at Aida. No one gave her a chance to speak in her own defence. After it was over, Aida was sent to prison for a whole year. Her crime was simply that she was a Christian.

Now that Aida knew just how hard it was to be a Christian, would she give it all up when she got out of prison, and settle down to an easier life? Aida knew that God loved her. And so she knew that she would do everything she could to stay loyal to him whatever happened.

It is always hard to get work when you have been in prison. The Russian authorities did all they could to make sure that, for Aida, it was doubly hard. For a short time she worked in a printing works but, after the police had caught her praying again, her employers said she must go. It was difficult, too, for Aida to find somewhere to live. She was not allowed to live in Leningrad and had to live with friends in a smaller town nearby. Then the police said she was not permitted to live there any more. They were determined to make her break the law so that they could put her in prison again.

Aida was in great danger. The police were hunting for her. When they found out where she was living, a plain clothes policeman followed her every move. One day, when she was out, they searched her room. There was the evidence they wanted! There were copies of the Christian magazines she had been sending out, as well as news about other Christians who had been sent to prison. For the third time in her life Aida found herself under arrest.

This time the authorities said Aida could defend herself at her trial.

'What shall I tell them?' she wondered. She knew that what she said would be important, not only for herself, but for other Christians too. It was hard to explain that she and the other Christians wanted to be loyal to the country they loved, but they had to be loyal to God first. If the law said they could not tell others about God, then they could not obey the law.

The courtroom was hushed. Everyone listened to what Aida had to say. The policemen were amazed by this slim young girl. She was so sure of her faith in God, so bold to speak up for him. Perhaps there was something in what she had to say? But they must not get sentimental. The trial was over and the prisoner must be punished. They marched Aida from the courtroom, and soon the heavy iron prison gates were closing behind her. Her three year prison sentence had begun.

Aida survived her three years in prison. She was

released in April 1971. However the authorities have apparently been preparing yet another case against her. Her story is not yet finished.

Aida, and the other people in this book, showed courage and loyalty inspired by God. Each of them when faced with a difficult or dangerous situation *put God first*.